Original title:
Tropical Light and Ocean Waves

Copyright © 2025 Creative Arts Management OÜ
All rights reserved.

Author: Benjamin Caldwell
ISBN HARDBACK: 978-1-80581-706-2
ISBN PAPERBACK: 978-1-80581-233-3
ISBN EBOOK: 978-1-80581-706-2

Ocean Symphony at Play

Seashells tapping like a band,
Coconuts rolling on the sand.
A fish in shades of bright confetti,
Dances to the waves, so unsteady.

Seagulls squawking out their tune,
While crabs are busting moves by the moon.
The waves are laughing, oh what a sight,
As sandcastles fall, a comical fright.

Emerald Shores Sparkling in the Glow

Green paradise, what a delight,
Where sunburns happen, what a fright!
Flip-flops flapping, people in cheer,
As sand gets stuck, oh dear, oh dear!

Beach balls bounce, a playful game,
Someone's lost a hat, oh what a shame!
Ice cream dripping, a sticky affair,
As kids chase after, without a care.

Celestial Crumbs on Sandy Paths

Stars fall like crumbs on the beach,
As jellyfish float, just out of reach.
Time to build a fort, with moats of goo,
Watch out for the tide—it's a sneaky undo!

Footprints leading to nowhere fast,
In flip-flops, I'm stumbling at last.
A wave crashes down, oh what a flap,
In the end, it's all just a splashy mishap!

Horizon's Embrace at Sunset's Call

The sky is blushing, a grin so wide,
While someone's trying to find a good tide.
With sunglasses on, we'll look so chic,
But in the water, we're all quite weak.

A sunset selfie, what a sight,
But wait! Is that sand in your bite?
Frolicking till the stars do appear,
Swaying to laughter, we cheer and cheer!

Daydreams in the Coastal Glow

Sandy toes and goofy grins,
Shells are hats for crabs and fins.
Seagulls dance with chips in tow,
Laughing hard, they steal the show.

Splashing waves, a silly fight,
Water guns will rule the night.
Flip-flops flying, what a sight,
Chasing laughter, pure delight.

Reveries of the Horizon's Embrace

Pineapple hats and fruit parade,
Sipping juice while jokes are made.
Surfboards wobble on a spree,
An octopus, oh let it be!

Sunscreen battles on the shore,
Pigeons plotting mischief more.
A crab retreats, a dance was done,
"Crustacean move!"—oh what fun!

Silhouetted Joy in Light's Caress

Shadows dance as day turns jest,
A sunburnt nose, a funny quest.
Tanned friends share a fishy tale,
While dolphins giggle in the gale.

Bamboo hats and slippery pages,
Silly tales of ancient sages.
A beach ball zooms from friend to foe,
Oops! There it goes—oh no, oh no!

Marvels of Dawn at the Water's Edge

Morning brings a giggle spree,
Seashells play hide and seek with glee.
Coffee spills, a splashy plot,
Laughter bursts—what a hot shot!

Paddleboards become a race,
Trying hard to find your place.
Fins come out in playful moods,
"Watch out for those sneaky food!"

Waves of Color on the Shining Sea

The sea is a canvas, splashed with hues,
A fish in a tux, asking for a cruise.
Seaweed dances, it knows the groove,
While crabs in the background break into a move.

A seagull strolls with a swagger so grand,
Stealing a fry from a sunbather's hand.
The sun's on vacation, just having a blast,
While the waves giggle, they're having a cast.

Sunlit Secrets Under the Palm Canopy

Under the palms where the shadows play,
The squirrels are gossiping about their day.
One steals a nut, another a chip,
While the parrots yell, 'Don't let it slip!'

Bananas are hanging, but none take a bite,
They're plotting a party; it's quite a sight.
The coconuts laugh, they can't take the heat,
As the pineapples sway, moving to a beat.

Traverse the Gleaming Shoreline

Strolling along where the sand meets the tide,
A crab waves hello, his friend is inside.
A beach ball bounces, it's round and it rolls,
While sunburnt tourists search for lost shoals.

Flip-flops are dancing, left behind on the track,
As children dig castles, then plan their attack.
The ocean's a postcard, with humor it brings,
As mermaids gossip about fish weddings and rings.

Reflections of Serenity and Salt

In a tide pool's mirror, the starfish pose,
While octopus artists create art with their toes.
The sea turtle sighs, wearing sunscreen with pride,
As the backdrop of laughter swells with the tide.

A dolphin appears, performing the twist,
Telling jokes to the fish, they can't resist.
With shells in their hands, beachcombers pretend,
That seashells are treasures that never will end.

Swaying Palms and Shimmering Dreams

In sandals lost, we hop and skip,
A coconut falls, it's quite a trip!
The sun burns bright, but we don't care,
We'll chase the seagulls, if they dare!

Brightly colored drinks in hand,
We dance around, a lively band.
Don't mind the sand stuck to our toes,
We'll laugh it off, as the ocean flows!

Brilliance Beneath the Azure Sky

A crab in sunglasses looks quite cool,
While we splash water, acting the fool.
The fish all giggle, their scales so bright,
As we dive in, they scatter in flight.

With flip-flops flapping, we race to the shore,
But end up tumbling, giggling for more.
Our laughter echoes, the waves jump high,
Who knew fun could make the seagulls shy?

Luminous Horizons and Wave-Crafted Stories

We build our castles, oh so grand,
Until the tide comes, oh how it spanned!
With each crashing wave, our dreams take flight,
As shells whisper secrets beneath the light.

A dolphin dives, puts on a show,
While we shout loudly, 'Hey, nice flow!'
With snacks that tumble from our hands,
We discover beachside bandit plans!

Coral Reflections in Twilight Glow

The sun dips low, a golden ball,
We try to catch it, but we just fall.
The tide pulls back, teasing our feet,
As crabs tell tales of their quick retreat.

With sandy hugs and salty giggles,
We spot a starfish, doing the wiggles.
As dusk rolls in, with stars so bright,
We dance with shadows, what a sight!

Waves that Sing Beneath the Stars

When fish wear hats and dance in pairs,
The ocean hums with laughter, and no one cares.
A crab in sunglasses struts with pride,
While jellyfish play hide and seek, side to side.

Those waves are poets, with rhymes so slick,
With every splash, they chant and tick.
They bubble and giggle, swirling with glee,
Under a moon that grins, just like me.

Sunbeams Play Amongst Driftwood

On driftwood logs, sunbeams skate,
They tease the gulls and celebrate.
A seal juggles shells with a wink and a nod,
While palm trees sway like a troupe of odd.

The sun shouts, 'Catch me!' with a golden cheer,
As parrots squawk jokes that only they hear.
With every bright glimmer, a giggle breaks free,
Nature's own circus for you and for me.

Celestial Glow of the Evening Sea

Stars drop candies on waves that spin,
A tugboat cheers, 'Let the fun begin!'
With each gentle wave, a new joke unfurls,
As fish tell tales of underwater pearls.

The moon pulls at tides with a teasing grin,
And crabs throw parties from dusk until din.
Each splash is laughter, each foam a cheer,
The evening sea giggles, let's all draw near!

Luminescent Breezes and Distant Shores

Breezes whisper secrets, with twirls and twirls,
They tickle the waves, and the sea just whirls.
A sea turtle spins like a dancer on stage,
While sandcastles tiptoe, they're full of rage!

The wind tosses shells into a game of tag,
With laughter that echoes, oh what a brag!
Each breeze a jester, with a playful tease,
In nature's grand show, there's fun with ease!

Glints of Gold on Aqua Crests

Sunshine winks at the waves,
They giggle and splash with glee,
A fish wears sunglasses and grins,
As crabs dance like they're free.

Pelicans dive for a snack,
Like missiles from the sky so bright,
They miss and just land in the soup,
Leaving everyone in delight.

Toward the shore, a turtle spreads,
His limbs flailing in a race,
But the jellyfish wobbles by,
With an elegant, goofy grace.

Seagulls squawk their playful tunes,
As shells tumble down the beach,
They gather in laughter-filled groups,
And steal all of our sunscreen each!

Moonlit Dances on Azure Waters

Under the stars, the goggles gleam,
As fish twirl in a waltz so grand,
The moon snickers at the scene,
While seaweed plays in the sand.

Crabs break out with silly moves,
Shaking their claws like they're wild,
Under the silvery glow above,
Even the starfish seems beguiled.

A dolphin pranks with leaps and flips,
Splashing the surfers in a spree,
They laugh until they wipe out hard,
No one's safe, not even me!

As night wraps the world in dreams,
The ocean hums a cheeky song,
With waves and whispers of the night,
It's a party where we all belong!

Brilliance of the Seafoam Waves

Foamy figures twist and crawl,
A ballet on the briny stage,
Each curl and tumble's a fair game,
The ocean laughs, it's all the rage.

A crab wears a tiny top hat,
Strutting pride in its little way,
While starfish clap their silly hands,
Holding a shell-based cabaret.

Seashells shout in gleeful tones,
As mermaids join the playful song,
They frolic in the salty breeze,
And giggle all day long.

Frolicking fishes form a band,
Playing tunes to the ocean's beat,
The sea's a dance floor for all,
Where laughter echoes with each feat!

Echoes of Light on Sandy Shores

Footprints chase the retreating tide,
Little ones sprint, with giggles bright,
A sandcastle with radish flags,
Hoping to win the royal fight.

The beach ball takes a flying leap,
Over a pair of tanned sunburns,
And dolphins cheer with silly yips,
As laughter fills our playful turns.

A seagull steals a sandwich bite,
With a flourish of feathery flair,
While kids scream, 'Hey, that's not yours!'
They plot revenge with icy stares.

The sun sets on our sandy feast,
Decorating all with orange hue,
As waves play peek-a-boo with day,
We chuckle, 'Is tomorrow too?'

Glistening Swells of the Afternoon

Waves are dancing, doing a jig,
Water tickles creatures small and big.
A crab in a tux, what a sight to see,
As dolphins serenade with glee.

The sun's a ball, too hot to hold,
Making mermaids' tales shine like gold.
Sandcastles crumble, a royal mishap,
As seagulls squawk, 'Want a snack? Snap!'

Floaties drift, in hues so bright,
While surfers search for their perfect flight.
A sunburned dad yells, 'I've lost my hat!'
And somewhere a dog chases a rat.

With flip-flops flying, laughter fills the air,
As kids steal ice cream, without a care.
Just a day of fun, with splashes and shrieks,
In our silly paradise, all laughter peaks.

Radiant Breezes and Ocean Melodies

A breeze sweeps in, with a playful tease,
It steals my hat, oh what a breeze!
Seagulls giggle, circling high,
As I chase my belongings, oh my, oh my!

Umbrellas huddle, a colorful crowd,
While beachgoers dance, feeling proud.
A fellow in shades, dripped in sun,
Sings off-key, oh what fun!

Sand gets everywhere, it's a messy affair,
In sandwiches and shoes, and tangled hair.
But laughter rings louder than any complaint,
As a child declares, "My foot's a paint!"

With conga lines chasing after waves,
Sunburned noses, the laughter paves.
Our hearts are full, under the sun's gleam,
Making memories more vivid than a dream.

Sunbeams Play Among Coastal Shadows

Sunbeams dance, a playful crowd,
While shadows stretch and feel so proud.
A beach ball flies, an awkward arc,
Landing in a teenager's snack, oh, what a lark!

Flip-flops flop, a humorous sound,
As shells flip over, turning around.
A guy in pink, what was he thinking?
Spills his drink, and now he's blinking!

Sandals squabble, who's on the scene?
A dog digs frantically, looking for cuisine.
But all he finds is a lost flip-flop,
And with a wag, he won't stop, won't stop!

As sunsets melt, in hues so fine,
We laugh at our mishaps, all entwined.
For every slip, every silly deed,
Is a story to tell, that's guaranteed!

The Golden Embrace of Dusk

Evening descends, the sky's a treat,
Casting shadows, oh, what a feat!
A crab in my flip-flop, causing a fuss,
But I wave it off - I don't need the bus!

The last surfer rides, with style and flair,
His balance is wobbly, but we don't care.
As we munch on tacos, the gulls steal a bite,
And we just laugh, what a silly sight!

Children chase fireflies, sparklers of light,
While adults sip drinks and feel quite bright.
A dad sings loudly, to everyone's glee,
As the kids giggle, wishing he'd flee.

The moon's coming out, it's quite a show,
Casting silver dreams on the waves below.
In this golden embrace, where the laughter stays,
We dance and we play, in twilight's rays.

Cascade of Colors in a Coastal Breeze

The sun spilled juice on the ocean's cake,
Seagulls danced like they were on a break.
Waves wore hats, so stylish and bright,
While shells took selfies, oh what a sight!

Beach balls bounced, a circus of fun,
Sandy toes wiggling, everyone on the run.
Flip-flops flying, a joyful parade,
Crabs in tuxedos, perfectly displayed!

Kites soaring high, they're chasing the breeze,
While dolphins giggle, swimming with ease.
A piña colada in a pineapple cup,
Celebration's here, so let's live it up!

With beach umbrellas making a parade,
And laughter echoing, never to fade.
As twilight colors the sky with delight,
We dance in the surf, under soft moonlight.

Shimmering Horizons at Dusk

As the sun dips low with a wink and a grin,
The horizon glows, like a game to begin.
Fishes wear tutus, twirling in glee,
While crabs do the cha-cha, oh can't you see!

Waves wear sparkles, like they're out for a show,
With starlit applause, tides ebb and flow.
Seashells gossip, gossiping loud,
While sea stars play hide and seek in a crowd!

Cocktails in coconuts, sipping with flair,
While wind whispers secrets, without a care.
Moonbeams flash lights; they're ready to play,
Making waves chuckle and splash all the way.

The sand gets tickled by tiny shore birds,
As sunset giggles, sharing its words.
A night full of magic and lighthouse beams,
We'll dance 'til we stumble, lost in our dreams.

Emerald Depths and Radiant Riptides

In waters so green, where giggles are found,
Mermaids play poker, with laughter abound.
Starfish wear glasses, reading the tide,
While fish in tuxedos do the moonwalk with pride!

Waves go whoosh, but the crabs stand firm,
Singing sea shanties, all with good charm.
A seashell's a phone, ringing off the hook,
With octopuses dialing, so take a good look!

Jellyfish float like balloons in the breeze,
As dolphins glide by, all set to tease.
Turtles in hats, all scruffy and cute,
While snorkelers giggle in bright-colored suits.

A treasure chest full of giggles galore,
With gold coins that jingle, "Oh, bring us more!"
In a sea of adventures, together we'll roam,
Exploring the depths, where whimsy finds home.

Coral Dreams in a Sun-Kissed Paradise

Coral castles rise up, made of candy and dreams,
Where creatures in tutus perform seaside schemes.
Starfish play catch with the driftwood they find,
While seagulls race bicycles, one of a kind!

An octopus chef serves ice cream so sweet,
With bubbles for sprinkles, it's quite the treat.
The surfboards gossip, sharing tales from afar,
Of shorelines and sunsets, where beach lovers are.

A sunburnt crab moans, "My shell's gone all red!"
As a clam rolls its eyes, "You'd should've just fled!"
With laughter infectious, the tides pull us in,
We revel in joy, where the fun will begin!

So here's to the splashes, the sunshine, the waves,
Let's dance with the dolphins, be carefree and brave.
In this vibrant retreat, where the ocean sings,
We'll celebrate life and all its wild flings!

Sunrise Whispers on Sandy Shores

A pinch of sun jumps out of bed,
To tease the waves with laughter's spread.
Sandcastles giggle, hats take flight,
As seagulls squawk, 'What's up? Delight!

Flip-flops race with a sandy friend,
Chasing crabs, oh joy, no end.
Shells play peek-a-boo in the sand,
While kids shout, 'This beach is grand!'

Kites swirl up, a colorful sight,
A coconut rolls; what a silly flight!
The sun paints smiles on every face,
Life's a beach—a wild ace of grace!

So let the waves toss shoes and pride,
As we surf the waves, nowhere to hide.
From sunup to sundown, let it flow,
With laughter and fun, let the good vibes grow!

Celestial Radiance over Aqua Mirrors

Stars wink at the bay with a splash,
While the moon's a glowstick in a flash.
Fish hold parties beneath the bright,
With bubbles and giggles, oh what a sight!

Skimmers in sunglasses strut like pros,
While jellyfish giggle and do their shows.
A sand crab with shades bluntly glares,
'Who invited the mermaids? It's not fair!'

Lanterns bob like jelly in the night,
Echoing laughter, a pure delight.
Shellfish hold tales of long-lost lore,
As the tide decides to dance on the shore.

So let the constellations guide the play,
With sparkles and antics that never sway.
Waves tickle toes, as jokes fly wide,
Under the stars, let's enjoy the ride!

The Dance of Sun-Kissed Waters

The sun twirls down like a ballerina,
Sipping cocktails from a coconut arena.
Surfboards dance to the beat of the sea,
While waves giggle, 'Come surf with me!'

Tanned toes tap to the ocean's beat,
As crabs join in with their own little feat.
Mermaids wink with a splash and swish,
While dolphins tease, 'Catch me if you wish!'

Sand buckets flip like they've lost their minds,
As the tide tickles toes, oh what fun it finds.
With splashes and laughter, we spin and roll,
In the warm embrace of the cheerful shoal!

So take a dip and lose all your cares,
Join in the fun; forget the stares.
For here in the warmth, we dance and play,
With laughter and joy, all through the day!

Illuminated Tides at Dusk

The day wraps up in colors so bold,
As sea turtles tell their tales of old.
Lanterns flicker as night starts to creep,
While beach balls bounce in a playful heap.

With sunset jokes and bright beach balloons,
The stars pop up like silly cartoons.
Waves roll in, tickling the shore,
'Is that a wave or a light-up chore?'

Balloons float high on a gentle breeze,
As the horizon smiles, oh what a tease!
Flip-flops fly as the music swells,
In a party where laughter truly dwells.

So grab a friend and join the fun,
Under the glow of the last setting sun.
With giggles and jests filling the air,
Let's make this dusk a memory to share!

Sun-Drenched Pathways to the Unknown

On a trail where flip-flops squeak,
Seagulls mock the sun, so cheeky,
Sandcastles dream of ocean's might,
While crabs throw parties in plain sight.

Waves munch on the salty shore,
Beach balls bounce as folks adore,
Sunscreen battles against the tan,
As one brave dog steals a picnic can.

Every towel tells a silly tale,
Of sunburned noses that go pale,
Frogs in shades croak out their pride,
Swimsuits scamper, too shy to hide.

In flip-flop warfare, a squawk will rise,
Underneath the bright, endless skies,
Laughter bubbles like the foamy brew,
As we chase the seagulls, just for a view.

Luminary Tides at the Turning Hour

As the sun winks at the sleepy shore,
A floating jellyfish starts to snore,
With every wave, a ticklish dance,
Seashells giggle in a merry trance.

The surfboards slide with a graceful flair,
While beach hats tumble in summer air,
Nudged by the tide, a sandwich dashes,
As crabs exchange their secret stashes.

At sunset's cue, the beach balls spree,
Costumed seagulls decide to flee,
While surfers chat in wild debate,
Over who's the best at catching bait.

Soon the moon arrives, all pajamas on,
Whispers of laughter till the dawn,
Mermaids laugh at the human plight,
In this spectacle of shimmering light.

Beachcomber's Muse under Golden Skies

With sunglasses perched upon my nose,
I chase a crab; oh, how it glows,
Shells discuss the gossip of the sea,
While my sunhat flies off, oh dear me!

Drifting by, a floatie takes its chance,
Socks and sandals join the dance,
A wave's grand scheme to steal my drink,
The beach is a stage, don't you think?

In search of treasures washed ashore,
I find a flip-flop, and then more,
A sunburned tourist starts to blog,
To write of crabs who sit and hog.

We trade our finds like silly kids,
As laughter spills like ocean's bids,
The golden hour wraps us tight,
In this quirky play of pure delight.

Horizon's Kiss at Daybreak

As dawn creeps in with a sleepy yawn,
The palm trees shake, a sunny brawn,
A flock of flamingos prance and sway,
Sing their morning songs—hey! No delay!

Chairs are arranged in a twinkling row,
Sandwiches plotting a sneaky show,
The waves take a splash and wipe the slate,
While my breakfast burrito can't wait!

Tanned folks tumble into morning thrill,
Strut their stuff with a confidence spill,
Coffee cups laugh at sleepy heads,
As circus seals roar in their beds.

A prankster wave gives a soggy kiss,
And steals my hat; oh, what bliss,
In this wild world of joy and play,
Every sunrise brings a brand-new day.

Elysian Ribbons of Light and Flow

In a hammock, I sway with glee,
Coconuts laughing, talking to me.
Sunbeams play tag on my nose,
While the seagulls decide to pose.

Bikinis all tangled in knots,
My flip-flops have fled to their spots.
Tanned toes dance in the sand,
While sunscreen is lost, oh, so grand!

Laughter erupts with each wave crash,
A sandcastle built, ready to smash.
My drink has a funny little umbrella,
Is it a beach or a fairytale fella?

Here comes the tide with a giggly tease,
It tickles my feet, oh, such a breeze!
Life's a fiesta, come join the fun,
Under the glow of a melting sun.

Enchanted Currents Beneath a Velvet Canopy

Under a canopy, shadows play,
Bananas waving in the soft sway.
A crab in a tux tries to waltz,
All while I'm lost in a salty somersault.

Jellyfish wiggling with fancy flair,
To a disco beat that's hardly fair.
I slip on a seaweed, it's quite a scene,
As fish laugh at my dance routine.

Palm trees whisper sweet, silly songs,
Calling to me as I twirl along.
Clouds shaped like dogs race through the sky,
I chuckle at how they seem to fly.

The tide rolls in, with a chuckle and grin,
Chasing my sandwich, oh what a sin!
With giggles and splashes, I join the parade,
In this magical land, fun's never delayed.

Breezy Wishes on Rippled Canvas

A kite took flight, but not my goal,
It tumbled down, into a pool of coal.
I dive in quick, now I'm all wet,
But oh! What a colorful silhouette!

Flip-flops go missing, where could they roam?
The seagulls decide to make them their home.
With a laughter that's bright, the sun gives chase,
While I grin wide, with salt on my face.

Ice cream drips, a psychedelic trail,
While I'm trapped in a sticky Fondant veil.
Mango flavors dance on my tongue,
A wobble and jig, oh, the song unsung!

But the ocean winks, as I tip and sway,
It's a giggling partner for every play.
Tickle the breeze, as the colors twirl,
In this joyful dance, let's give it a whirl!

Celestial Diamonds on Salted Waves

Stars fall like confetti in the night,
While crabs want to dance, oh what a sight!
They moonwalk in rhythm, sideways in style,
With twinkling shells, they pose and smile.

A boat's rocking, with a pirate's cheer,
Playing sea shanties, but on a leer.
Tiny dolphins leap, as if on a dare,
Riding the waves like they just don't care!

Moonlit waves have a mischievous gleam,
Whispering secrets like a sweet dream.
My flip-flop floats, a shipwreck relic,
Is it a joke, or just pure magic?

The tide giggles, with a splish and a splash,
As I join in, with a belly laugh crash.
On this crazy coast, where smiles collide,
Even the ocean has nothing to hide!

Serenades of Surf Beneath Starlit Skies

Waves do the cha-cha on sandy floors,
While curious crabs tap dance on the shores.
Seagulls sing karaoke, with style and flare,
Their outfits are wild, oh what a rare affair!

The moon chuckles softly, up high and above,
As turtles attempt their best dance moves of love.
A starfish DJs, spinning shells with delight,
While jellyfish glow, it's a colorful night!

Sandcastles giggle in the shimmering breeze,
Tickled by tides that swirl with such ease.
Laughter erupts from each bubbling crest,
As crabs in tuxedos declare it a fest!

The laughter rolls in with the playful tide,
Each splash a new joke the ocean has spied.
Under the starlight, life's show must go on,
With waves full of whimsy until the dawn!

The Allure of Crimson Sundowns

Sunset's a painter, with hues oh so bold,
Mixing oranges with pinks, a masterpiece told.
Fish flip and flop, joining in on the fun,
While seagulls shout, 'Hey, look at that one!'

Palm trees lean in like they're sharing a joke,
Whispering secrets of the waves' playful yoke.
The horizon blushes, a funny old chap,
Stealing the show in a colorful wrap!

As the sun takes a bow, the crowd gives a cheer,
Dolphins bob up, making it loud and clear.
Their flips are a spotlight, a daring display,
While crabs on the rocks just laugh and sway.

With giggles and chuckles, day bids adieu,
A sunset soirée, really quite the view.
Stars peek through, and they giggle as well,
At the spectacle of nature's curious spell!

Rolling Emotions in Nature's Embrace

Waves tumble and roll, just like a big cat,
Chasing sandcastles that look like a hat.
Otters play tag, with mischief in tow,
While crabs hold a meeting, plotting their show!

The tides throw a party, it's quite a blast,
With seashells as snacks and the fish swimming fast.
A dolphin brings jokes, oh, what a delight,
As the sun winks at clouds, 'Just hang on tight!'

Fishes flip-flop like they're in a spree,
With seaweed confetti, it's a jubilee.
The sea breeze giggles, tickling your nose,
As the tides dance together, everybody knows!

The joy rolls ashore, a wave of pure glee,
Where each splash is laughter from the deep sea.
Nature tips her hat to this rollicking play,
With waves that keep chuckling all through the day!

Sunlit Reflections on Cerulean Tides

In a pool of laughter, the ocean's a king,
With surfboards as chariots, ready to swing.
Seagulls wear shades, and the crabs rock their ties,
In this sunny parade under bright azure skies!

The waves tap dance, making ripples of fun,
Inviting the sun to join in their run.
Bubbles burst out with a giggle and splash,
As fish hold a contest for the biggest crash!

The sand grumbles softly, 'Hey, keep it down!',
While the dolphins throw flips, as they swim all around.
With shells as their crowns, they crown the best jest,
In this summer kingdom, the joy's at its best!

When sunset arrives, it's a magical sight,
As colors explode, making laughter take flight.
From whispers to roars, the ocean's a friend,
With waves full of chuckles, that never shall end!

Shimmers of Serenity in the Breeze

The seagulls are dabbing sunscreen on their beaks,
While beach balls roll, pretending to be sleek.
Flip-flops are flapping like they're on a spree,
And sandy toes wiggle, wearing joy like a spree.

The sunbeams are giggling, tickling our nose,
As laughter erupts, like popcorn it goes.
Cool drinks in hand, we're quite the sight,
Sipping on fun in the golden sunlight.

Crabs in their shells wear tiny sun hats,
Trying to dance in their poofy spats.
Seashells are chatting in their sassy tone,
While dolphins' pranks get everyone's tone.

Breezy tunes weave through swaying palms,
Every joke just adds to our charms.
As waves roll in with a playful cheer,
We laugh together, our worries disappear.

Echoes of Laughter on Sunlit Beaches

Kites soaring high, look like fish in the air,
While munching on snacks without a care.
Sandcastles crumble with giggles and glee,
The king of the beach is a crab, can't you see?

With sunglasses on, we pose like pros,
Pointing at seashells, pretending they glow.
The tide brings in treasures, they're mostly just goo,
But we cheer like we found something brand new.

Seagulls squawk gossip about folks on the run,
As splashes and chortles add to the fun.
In this bright paradise, we wiggle and roll,
Sharing a laugh, that's the ultimate goal.

The flavor of watermelons dripping in sun,
Is rivaled by laughter—can it be outdone?
As sunsets paint the sky in a fairy tale hue,
We know that tomorrow brings more laughter too.

Vibrant Palettes of Seafoam and Sky

Colors collide like kids at a fair,
With beach towels spreading without a care.
Sun hats ask questions while floaties just grin,
As jellyfish dance, inviting us in.

Pineapple slices hold secrets so sweet,
Chased by wave frogs on their frantic feet.
A splash turns to giggles as someone slips by,
We all burst out laughing, oh me, oh my!

The horizon wears stripes of pink and gold,
While surfboards wait, looking brave and bold.
Roasted marshmallows stacked way too high,
As shadows grow long, we can't help but sigh.

Every moment a canvas, painted with cheer,
From the echoing waves we hold so dear.
As sunset chuckles, day drifts into night,
Our fun-filled escapades bathe in starlight.

Whispers of the Sea under a Glorious Sky

The breeze is a joker, tickling our chins,
While sunscreens battle to cover our skins.
Flip-flops are racing, oh, what a sight,
As shadows of palm trees dance with delight.

The ocean hums tunes of old sailor lore,
While jellyfish juggle, we beg them for more.
A pirate's hat scarecrow guards all the snacks,
As kids sail their dreams on inflatable hacks.

Footprints in sand tell tales of the day,
As laughter and whispers drift far, they play.
Seashells collecting our wishes and woes,
At sunset, we gather like blooms in a row.

Underneath starlight, we count every wave,
Tickling each other—oh, how we crave,
To keep this sweet chaos, our magical spree,
Captured forever, just you and me.

Serenity Found in Shimmering Waves

In the sun's dance, jellyfish glide,
Amongst flip-flops, we take a ride,
Seagulls steal chips, they make such a scene,
Laughter echoes where water's serene.

The sunburned tourist, a sight to behold,
In a mix of pink and silver, quite bold,
Splashing around like a fish on a spree,
While sunscreen battles the wild, salty sea.

Waves crash like laughter, a bubbling tune,
As crabs plot their escape with a humorous swoon,
Beach balls go flying, oh what a joy,
As kids build wet castles, they're proud of their ploy.

The hammock sways with a zig and a zag,
As the friendly coconut poses a gag,
A school of fish giggles, swims without care,
In a world where joy and chaos declare.

Embrace of the Coastal Breeze Beneath the Sun

The sand's a bit gritty, but our spirits are high,
With a flip of a towel, the seagulls all fly,
Sipping cold drinks while the sun shines bright,
We laugh at the beach bum who's lost in delight.

The beach ball bounces, chaos in its flight,
Whirling around, like a dance of pure fright,
While sun hats take flight, an unplanned ballet,
As surfboards collide, in a comical way.

Ice cream drips down, what a sticky plight,
But a sticky situation can feel just right,
We chase after laughter, let worries all flee,
In the breeze of the coast, oh what joy to be free!

Then there's the fellow who dives with great flair,
But he's left with a splash that extends through the air,
A chorus of giggles erupts from the shore,
As we revel in laughter, craving much more!

Kisses of Warmth on Water's Edge

The sun wraps us up in a warm, sandy hug,
While tourists trip over a beach towel jug,
Flip-flops are flying, laughter's the theme,
We're wise with our smiles, like a bright sunny dream.

The ocean waves whisper the secrets of fun,
As kids build tall castles, but then they all run,
A sudden wave crashes, what an uproar,
As laughter erupts, splashing things we adore.

The man with the grill, he's flipping a feast,
While trying to juggle, he's chasing a beast,
A seagull swoops low for a daring old snack,
And we watch as his tongs make a great little crack.

The warmth of the sands embraces our feet,
While beachgoers dance to a rhythm so sweet,
With each wave that splashes, comes joy and a grin,
As we soak in the laughter, let the fun begin!

Mirage of Light over the Sea's Embrace

In the shimmer and glow, the horizon's a game,
Where sun hats get tumbled and everyone's tame,
The ocean waves giggle, they roar and they crash,
While sunscreen attempts the impossible splash.

Paddleboards wobble, our balance a joke,
As laughter erupts like an old-fashioned cloak,
We chase after seaweed, it's forever in flight,
With dainty sea critters, oh what a sight!

The dance of the waves strains our rickety boat,
As someone yells, "Quick! Let's get back afloat!"
But we're tangled in joy, not a care in our heart,
As the ocean embraces, we don't want to part.

So here on this canvas, with laughter we paint,
The mirage of joy, with a pinch of complaint,
Underneath all the splashes, the fun never fades,
In the warmth of the waves, where happiness wades.

Reflections of Radiance and Ripples

Sun hats bobbing like boats in a race,
Laughter erupts with the sun on our face.
Seagulls perform their dive-bomb ballet,
Chasing our snacks that just flew away.

Shadows dance on the soft, golden sand,
Kids are on quest for the biggest clams they planned.
A crab in a hurry, a flip and a dash,
Stealing our lunch in a sea-salt splash!

Chasing Daylight along the Shore

Surfboards wobble as we take our stance,
A tumble, a splash, a comical chance.
Seashells giggle as they play hide-and-seek,
While the tide rolls in with a whimsical squeak.

Footprints trailing like a chaotic spree,
Chasing the waves that whisper to me.
A sunscreen battle, slippery and bright,
Goes on between friends till there's no more light.

Glimmering Shallows in a Radiant Day

Bubbles pop under the sun's warm touch,
Fish wearing sunglasses, oh, that's too much!
Diving for treasures that aren't really there,
Finding old flip-flops, what a wacky affair.

Turtles in flip-flops are winning this race,
While jellyfish jiggle with grace and with pace.
A splash in the face brings laughter and cheer,
As we soak in the fun, our troubles unclear.

Allure of Aqua Hues and Golden Rays

A beach ball drifts like a sailor afloat,
Paddling kids on their inflatable boat.
Sunscreen glistens in a fruity swirl,
As seagulls watch on, giving us a twirl.

The sandcastle king, with a crown made of goo,
Declares it's snack time; it's pizza for two!
We munch on the beach while the waves play their tune,
Under the watchful eye of a happy raccoon.

Luminous Shores Beneath a Golden Sky

Seagulls laughing at the crabs,
Doing the limbo on the sand.
Sunscreen battles, a slippery game,
Falling like fish, oh isn't it grand?

Flip-flops flying, a great big splash,
Chasing after waves like silly kids.
An octopus joins in the dance,
Wiggling arms, look at those bids!

A sandcastle with a lopsided throne,
The seashells grinning at the sight.
Mermaids giggle, their hair a mess,
Stealing snacks, oh what a delight!

The sun dips low, a golden crown,
All creatures call it a day.
With laughter echoing from the bay,
The tide waves goodbye, in a cheerful way!

Whispering Currents and Dappled Sunbeams

The waves are whispering silly jokes,
While surfers try to catch a ride.
Each tumble brings a splashy laugh,
As they roll like fish, full of pride!

Colorful flip-flops on rainbow feet,
Making fashion statements in the sea.
A beach ball bounces, dodging faces,
Oh what a sight, pure jubilee!

Sandy sandwiches are set to fly,
With toppings that never quite fit.
A seagull swoops, snatches a fry,
Chaos ensues, everyone is a bit hit!

Dappled shadows dance on cheeky toes,
As laughter blends with salty spray.
Who knew the ocean had such flair?
It's a party every single day!

Radiance on the Horizon's Edge

Each sunset paints a giggling scene,
As dolphins leap with a flirty grin.
The horizon whispers its bright secrets,
While piña coladas spin within.

Sandy cheeks and sunglasses askew,
Every beachgoer rocking their best.
With beach balls colliding in glorious chaos,
It's a wild, wacky, sandy fest!

Shells are rolling like wayward cars,
Chasing laughter on the shore.
A crabs' parade winks at the crowd,
Old as they are, they still want more!

As the stars begin to twinkle bright,
All creatures join in a silly dance.
With footprints left in a giggly night,
Who needs sleep when you have romance?

Dance of the Glimmering Surf

The silver waves are full of glee,
It's a splash zone, come take your spot.
Seashells spinning, hula hoop fun,
As the sun beams down, connecting the dots.

A crab attempts a moonwalk strut,
While jellyfish prance with a glowing flair.
Waves cascade in rhythmic beats,
Making seaweed twirl in salty air!

Young and old join in the show,
As laughter harmonizes with the tide.
Flip and flop, it's a wild rave,
No one can hide from the ocean's ride!

As the day ebbs away like warm sand,
Fireflies jive in the glow of the moon.
In this dance of playful glee,
We'll return for the surf, oh so soon!

Flora Weaving with the Gentle Breeze

Daisies dance with the soft air,
While cacti wear hats, oh so rare.
Palm trees giggle in pretty sway,
As lizards play hide and seek all day.

Mossy rocks wearing fuzzy green,
Whispering secrets, laughing in between.
A coconut rolls, causes a stir,
"Watch out!" yells a crab, in quite a blur.

Seashells wink, they think they're sly,
Each one a treasure, oh me, oh my!
Anemones wave like they're at a ball,
In this riot of nature, we're having a ball.

Laughter echoes through colors so bright,
As the sun sneezes, giggling in delight.
Here in this garden, with sunlight so free,
Nature's a clown, come join the spree!

Cascading Colors of the Shoreline

The sand tickles toes, oh what a tease,
While seaweed wigs wave in the breeze.
Pebbles roll like marbles, round and free,
Each wave whispers, "Come play with me!"

Crabs in a conga line, quite the sight,
Bouncing along, feeling just right.
Starfish do the limbo, quite low,
As shells join the party, putting on a show.

Seagulls squawk jokes as they dive for a treat,
While the beach ball is bouncing by happy feet.
Bright umbrellas bloom like flowers in June,
Laughing under the warm afternoon moon.

Sandcastles smile with icing on top,
As waves give a nod, then decide to stop.
Colors collide, like they're painting a dream,
In this funny world, laughter's the theme!

Tidepool Treasures in Silver Light

Bubbles giggle as they dance up high,
Tiny fish peek, and the sea stars sigh.
Mollusks wear hats, though they're a bit tight,
In the puddles of wonder, shimmering bright.

A starfish twirls like a fancy ballerina,
While hermit crabs plot, like they're in a subpoena.
Sea cucumbers lounge and take a load off,
While whispering secrets and giggling soft.

Jellyfish jive in their gelatinous ways,
While snails tell stories of long, winding days.
Barnacles wave with their barnacle flair,
In this quirky kingdom where we all share.

A splash from a wave gets everyone wet,
Then seaweed starts tickling, oh what a pet!
In the silver light, treasures of fun,
The ocean's a clown, and we're on the run!

Dappled Sun on the Rolling Waves

The sun licks the waves, oh what a tease,
While squawking gulls hang by with ease.
Surfboards waltz in the foamy ballet,
As surfers tumble, it's the funniest play!

The sunbeam giggles, gets stuck in a swirl,
As beach balls bounce, giving a twirl.
Kites fly high, tangled in trees,
While the beach blanket flops with the breeze.

Fins pop up, dance in the gleam,
Each splash creates quite the humorous scene.
As laughter rolls like the waves so grand,
Join the fun, it's a sun-soaked band!

A crab wears sunglasses, what a sight!
And shells play the trumpet, feeling just right.
With dappled sun shining, it's quite the craze,
In this jovial world of rolling waves!

Waves of Color beneath Sunlit Auras

In the splash of hues, the surf does dance,
A fish in shades of pink wears a funny stance.
Seagulls gossip, flying round with glee,
While crabs in tuxedos sip coconut tea.

Bubbles pop like jokes, they scatter with cheer,
As sunbeams giggle, it's crystal clear.
The ocean's palette, a painter's delight,
Sprays watercolors from morning to night.

Flip-flops chase children, giggling they run,
A sandcastle wears a crown, oh what fun!
Waves whisper secrets to the golden shore,
While sun hats roll off, wanting to explore.

So here we frolic, in this canvas bright,
Crafting stories where objects take flight.
With laughter and waves, the colors confess,
That life is a joke, and we're here to bless.

Glistening Retreats where Sun Meets Sea

Palm trees sway like dancers in a show,
While sunscreen battles won't steal the glow.
Shells conspire, plotting a slippery prank,
As waves crash in laughter, filling the tank.

A beach ball escapes, it's on the run,
Chasing a toddler, oh what silly fun!
Flip-flops abandon their comfy routine,
As toes dive deep in the foamy sheen.

Ice cream cones drip in a sticky plight,
While seagulls wheel in a comic flight.
Sandcastles topple with laughter and cheer,
As pint-sized pirates draw treasure maps here.

Coconuts giggle beneath the bright rays,
Crafting mock tales of the sunniest days.
So let's toast to joy, in this shimmering swell,
For sunsets and giggles, we know all too well.

Fables of the Dune and Dappled Sun

The dunes recount tales in a sun-drenched hum,
While lizards in sunglasses wiggle and strum.
Footprints swirl like a dance on the sand,
As laughter ricochets across this land.

Kites soar like dreams in electric blue skies,
While a whale sings ballads, oh what a surprise!
Octopuses juggle, entrancing all near,
As starfish retell the tales of good cheer.

Buckets and spades now move with intent,
Constructing odd figures and art with no rent.
The shells play with echoes of laughter so pure,
Creating a symphony we all can endure.

At dusk the horizon ignites with pure glee,
As we sit by the shore, sipping sweet tea.
The fables spun here, like shells in a line,
Reveal that fun waits where the sun likes to shine.

Mirthful Sojourns in Bright Embrace

A hammock sways low, cradling the sun,
While sunglasses sparkle, oh what blissful fun.
A seahorse rides waves, doing flips in the foam,
While beachgoers giggle, feeling quite at home.

Flippers take flight, as laughter flows wide,
As sunscreen battles become a strange ride.
Waves splash in chorus, a rhythmic delight,
While sand does its jig under the moonlight.

A crab in a hat, oh what a fine sight,
Challenges gulls to a frolicsome fight.
The ocean's enchantment, a carnival thrill,
Where smiles and joy blend, all laughter to spill.

So let's raise our shells in this frolicsome spree,
To friendship and fun, and the laughter of sea!
For every bright moment, we treasure with glee,
In this realm of wonders, forever we'll be.

Lush Landscapes Bathed in Sunlight

In a garden where the laughter grows,
Silly squirrels put on their showy clothes.
Parrots squawk with flair and delight,
While ants march on, a parade in sight.

The sunbeam tickles every leaf,
A giggling flower, oh what a motif!
Chasing shadows, they jive with grace,
Nature's dance, an amusing race.

Coconuts crack jokes on the trees,
As the breeze joins in with giddy tease.
Even the sand seems tickled pink,
Winking along, it makes you think.

So come and frolic in this fun spree,
Where the wild things be and the sun's so free.
Laughter echoes in this vibrant bloom,
A quirky world, where joy finds room.

Harmony of the Ocean's Gentle Glow

Waves that laugh as they hit the shore,
Ticklish tides that want to explore.
Starfish pose on sandy beds,
Winking at crabs with silly threads.

The pufferfish poofs with glee,
While schools of fish toss confetti!
Seagulls strut with honks that jest,
Wearing funny hats, they're quite the fest.

With every splash, a giggle sings,
As dolphins leap and do funny things.
A jellyfish sways like a noodle,
Making waves dance, oh what a doodle!

So let your worries drift with the foam,
Join the jesters, make this place your home.
In this watery land of charm and cheer,
You'll find laughter, loud and clear.

Serenade of the Shimmering Coast

The sun winked at the sands today,
It's a masterpiece in a silly array.
Shells gather round for a cheeky chat,
About the crab who wore a hat!

Mermaids giggle, tossing their hair,
While fish wear sunglasses with cosmic flair.
A laugh rings out from the coral spree,
'Fishy fashion is the key, you'll see!'

With every wave, a joke does swell,
A tale of a clam who fell and fell.
He opened wide, a pearl of wit,
When the tide came in, he wasn't fit!

So dance on the shore, let your spirit soar,
Join the chorus of giggles galore.
In this shimmering playground of fun,
The serenade has just begun!

Trails of Light on the Open Waves

Oh, the trails that shimmer like a spool,
Sailing through giggles is the best rule.
Here comes a boat with a giant grin,
Full of laughter and a little spin.

The captain's hat is on a seal,
He's the one steering with zest and zeal.
A parrot yells, 'Look at me fly!'
As the waves bubble up with a sigh.

Splashing about like a bunch of fools,
Surfboards dance; the ocean schools.
With every ride comes a hearty cheer,
As the humor flows crystal clear.

So set your sails and join the fun,
Under the rays of a playful sun.
Count the laughs as they sail the bay,
In this world where joy rules the day.

Luminous Echoes Along the Coastline

Seagulls squawk, doing their dance,
Sandy toes get every chance.
A crab scurries with a shell on tight,
Chasing waves in midday light.

Flip-flops squeak on sun-warmed ground,
As beach balls bounce, oh what a sound!
A sunhat flies, oh what a sight,
Chasing it down feels just right.

Umbrellas tilt like hats askew,
While sunscreen's smeared in a messy zoo.
Laughter echoes, ripples of cheer,
As ice cream drips, we hold it near.

The tide rolls in and the tide rolls out,
Jellyfish don't care, they twist about.
With every splash, we shout with glee,
Summer fun, just you and me.

Isles of Wonder by the Quiet Sea

Floating thoughts like coconut boats,
Swimmy fish wear tiny coats.
A parrot squawks, "Who stole my snack?"
While waves giggle, "We'll get it back!"

Shells on my toes, oh what a find,
A starfish grins, I swear it's blind.
Palms sway with a breeze so sweet,
As sunburned noses parade down the street.

A sandcastle rises with a puff,
But watch your step, oh boy, it's rough!
The tide decides to join the fun,
And soon it's gone, oh how we run!

Under the sun, we're silly and free,
Making memories, just you and me.
So let's ride the waves, don't be shy,
In this carefree splash, let's touch the sky.

Whispering Light through Verdant Veils

Lemons roll like beach balls near,
As laughter drips like soda gear.
Vines entwine and play their game,
While lizards bask without a shame.

Palm fronds flutter, like they've got style,
Each giggle lengthens out a mile.
Bananas don't swing, they dance instead,
While toucans croon while turning red.

Hammocks swing, and giggles blend,
Gentle breezes start to send.
Oh look at that! A monkey climbs,
In search of snacks, and funky rhymes.

A splash of juice, a dribble here,
Cocktails served with cheerful cheer.
So let's roll in the sun today,
Where joy and silliness always play.

www.ingramcontent.com/pod-product-compliance
Lightning Source LLC
Chambersburg PA
CBHW072133070526
44585CB00016B/1655